ONCE UPON A TIME IN CHINA

THE
PIRATE
KING

JILLIAN LIN
Illustrations by SHI MENG

*Koxinga (Zheng Chenggong),
pirate and army leader (1624–1662)*

Once upon a time in China...

... lived a very powerful pirate. He had a son called Koxinga, who lived in Japan with his mother. When the boy turned seven, his mother called him to her side.

'Son,' she said, 'your father wants you to move to China so you can go to school there.'

'I don't want to!' Koxinga cried. 'I want to stay here with you.'

'You'll have to go alone,' his mother said. 'Women are not allowed to leave Japan, and I'm too poor to send you to a good school here.'

Koxinga had no choice and soon found himself on a ship bound for China. The trip took ten days.

Every night, he stood staring towards the east where he came from, with tears in his eyes.

When he arrived, Koxinga found out life was very different in China. His father turned out to be very rich. Not only was he an admiral in the emperor's navy, but he also had a large fleet of pirate ships. He earned more than 100,000 silver taels a year. Today, this would be more than 50 million dollars.

Not surprisingly, Koxinga got to live in a castle. It was surrounded by gardens with fountains, fishponds, and even a small zoo. His father hoped he would get a good job in the government and not become a pirate like him.

So he hired private teachers who taught Koxinga everything about Chinese culture and history. From his uncles he learnt how to ride a horse and fight with a sword. Koxinga worked very hard, and his teachers said, 'This boy is both clever and brave.'

Even though Koxinga had a good life, he missed his mother very much. He had not seen her for many years. When she could finally travel out of Japan, he was already a grown-up man.

Koxinga was excited to meet his mother again after such a long time. A short while before she arrived, however, he heard some bad news.

The Manchu people from the north had bumped the emperor off his throne as part of their plan to take over China. Koxinga's father tried to help by keeping the emperor safe.

Soon, the whole family started fighting against the Manchu people.

One day, his father received a letter. It said,

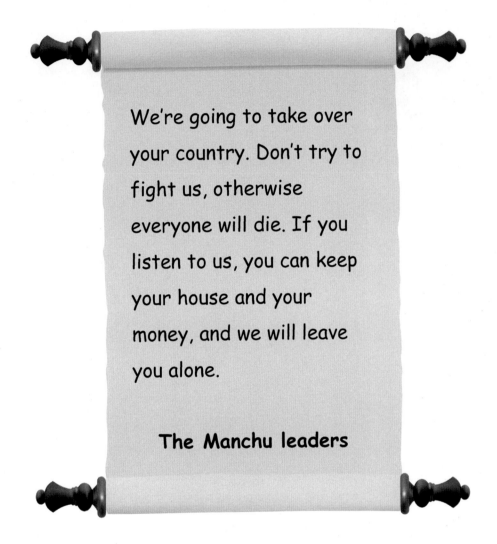

We're going to take over your country. Don't try to fight us, otherwise everyone will die. If you listen to us, you can keep your house and your money, and we will leave you alone.

The Manchu leaders

Koxinga's father got scared and told the family, 'Stop fighting! Let the Manchus in.'

At that time, Koxinga's mother had just made it into China. But before Koxinga could see her, the Manchus attacked the town she was in. His mother got killed.

Worse still, the Manchus broke their word against his father. Instead of leaving him and his family alone, they threw his father in prison.

When Koxinga found out, he was both sad and angry. 'I hate the Manchus! We can't let them take over our country. I will fight for China. I will get China back from those monsters,' he said.

The rest of the family agreed with him so Koxinga became the new leader of the family.

They immediately started to fight the Manchus.
Koxinga built up a huge fleet of war ships which he
used to attack towns and fortresses along the coastline.
To pay for weapons and food for his men, he forced
ships that were passing by to hand over their money.
So Koxinga became a pirate, just like his father.

At first, Koxinga and his men won all the battles against the Manchus. He decided to march north with his troops to retake the city of Nanjing. His soldiers camped around the city walls for two weeks.

'Let's attack now,' said his soldiers. Koxinga shook his head. 'We'll wait here until they run out of food and give up. That way, no one will get killed.' But he had made the wrong decision.

In the middle of the night, one of his soldiers secretly climbed the city walls. He told the Manchus on the other side what the weak spots in Koxinga's camp were.

The Manchus immediately started digging tunnels. After a few days, they crawled through them and attacked Koxinga's army. The soldiers were not prepared so the Manchus won the battle. Koxinga had to run for his life.

Even though many of his soldiers were killed, Koxinga didn't give up. He decided to look for a place to hide and build up a new army. He found an island not far from China. The only problem was that people from Holland lived on the island. They also had guns. However, Koxinga was not afraid. He told the Dutch people, 'Give yourselves up. You will lose the fight against me. I have the power to move heaven and earth.

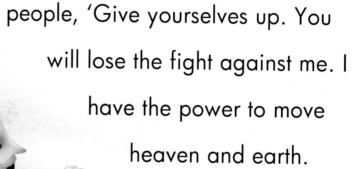

Wherever I go, I will win.'

The Dutch did not listen. They said, 'Those Chinese are cowards. They are scared of our guns. Once we shoot our guns, they'll be running for their lives.'

Koxinga got his warships ready and started the attack. He got 25,000 men from China to board his ships. When Koxinga's men landed on the island, the Dutch knew they were outnumbered and soon gave themselves up.

Koxinga became the king of the island, which we now know as Taiwan.

Unfortunately, Koxinga wasn't king for very long. Five months later, he was bitten by mosquitoes and died of the malaria disease.

His son became king for the next twenty years until the Manchus took over the island.

Sadly, Koxinga's dream of winning against the Manchus did not come true. However, he became a hero to the Chinese as well as the Japanese.

In Taiwan, hundreds of temples, schools, and centres are named after him. In other parts of southeast Asia, people also worship and pray to him.

His father should not have worried about his son becoming a pirate. Koxinga became the only pirate in the world who some people look up to as a king, a hero, and a god.

The End

1 ~ Koxinga means 'The Lord of the Imperial Surname'. The Chinese emperor gave him this title as a reward for his help. In China he is also known as 'Zheng Chenggong' and in Japan as 'Kokusen'ya'.

2 ~ Some people described Koxinga as being pale, scarred and handsome with fast-moving eyes and pointed teeth. He used to yell wildly in battle and was deadly with his samurai sword as well as his bow and arrow.

3 ~ After his mother's funeral, Koxinga went to a Confucian temple where he burned his scholarly robes (his school uniform). He prayed, 'In the past I was a good student and a good son. Now I'm an orphan without an emperor. I have no country and no home. My father has surrendered himself to the Manchus. My only choice is to fight against them and let my father down. Please forgive me.'

Statue of Koxinga inside his shrine in Tainan City, Taiwan.

Statue of the Dutch surrendering to Koxinga in Taiwan.

4 ~ When Koxinga reached the city of Nanjing, he wrote little notes asking the city leaders to give themselves up. He tied them to arrows that he shot into the city.

5 ~ The Manchus put Koxinga's father to death when Koxinga continued to fight against them and refused to give up.

6 ~ As soon as Koxinga landed in Taiwan, the Dutch soldiers marched toward the much larger enemy force with their guns. They fired three shots. Instead of running away, as the Dutch had expected, Koxinga's soldiers let loose so many arrows that the sky grew dark. Koxinga also sent a group of soldiers to sneak behind the Dutch. It wasn't long before he was able to crush the Dutch enemy.

7 ~ In Taiwan, the portraits and statues of Koxinga show him as a noble lord in ordinary clothes. His small beard makes him look serious and important. There is only one memorial of Koxinga in China. It is a statue of him on Gulangyu Island in the southern province of Fujian. Dressed in military uniform, he gazes across the water towards the island of Taiwan.

8 ~ One of the leading universities in Taiwan, National Cheng Kung University, is named after Koxinga.

9 ~ Famous Japanese playwright Chikamatsu
Monzaemon wrote a puppet play about Koxinga.
It became his most popular play.

10 ~ You can find a statue of Koxinga as a child
together with his mother in Tainan City, Taiwan.
It is located in the family shrine built by Koxinga's
son in honor of his father.

1   Why did Koxinga have to leave his mother and move to China?

a)   Because his father wanted him to go to school there.

b)   Because he was sick of living in Japan and wanted to see more of the world.

c)   Because he wanted to learn horseriding and swordfighting.

2   What did Koxinga's father do to make sure his son wouldn't turn into a pirate?

a)   He locked Koxinga up in his room and made him read books.

b)   He taught him horseriding so he wouldn't want to go on a ship.

c)   He hired private teachers for him to learn culture and history.

Answers to the Quiz: 1. a / 2. c / 3. b / 4. c / 5. b

3   Why did Koxinga decide to fight against the Manchus?

a)   Because his father and the rest of his family told him to.

b)   Because the Manchus had killed his mother and threw his father in prison.

c)   Because the Manchus had taken over the palace he was living in.

4   Why didn't Koxinga attack the city of Nanjing, but camped outside the walls instead?

a)   He was tired from his journey north.

b)   He wanted to have a nice dinner first.

c)   He didn't want anyone to get killed.

5   How did Koxinga beat the Dutch on the island of Taiwan, even though they had guns?

a)   He used a lot of arrows to chase them away.

b)   He outnumbered the Dutch with his 25,000 men.

c)   He told the Dutch that he would win against them.

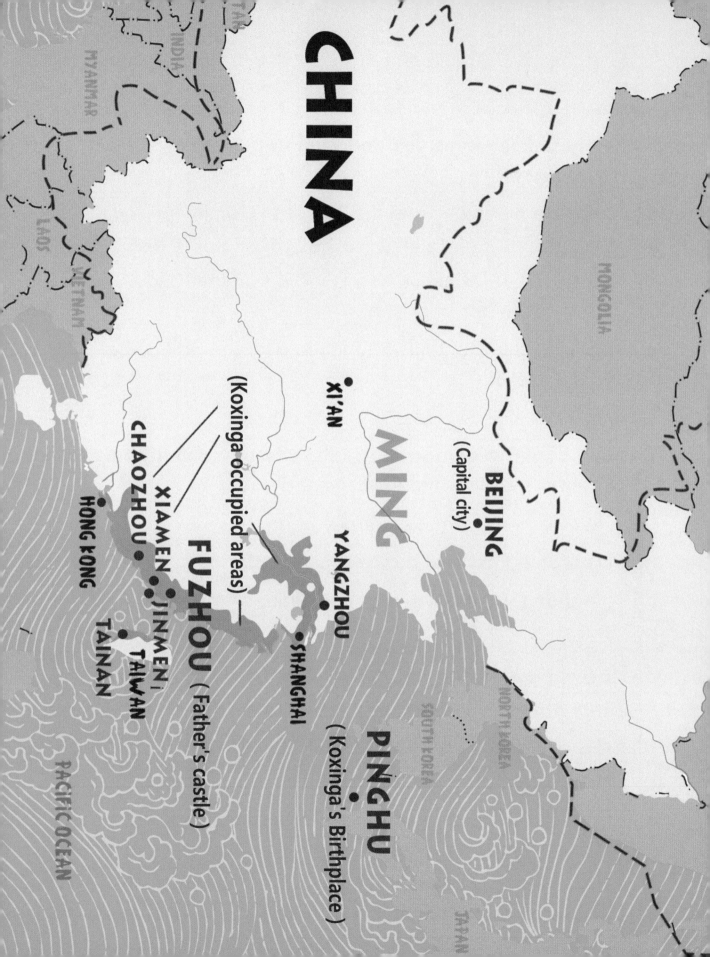

The *Once Upon A Time In China...* Series

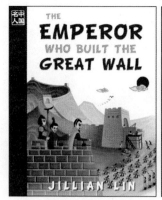
Qin Shihuang

Confucius

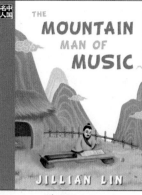
Zhu Zaiyu

Hua Tuo

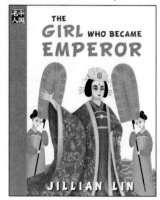
Wu Zetian

Zhang Heng

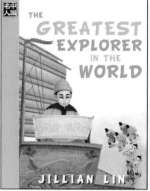
Zheng He

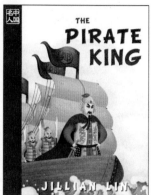
Koxinga

Also available as e-books. For more information, visit

www.jillianlin.com

The Pirate King

Copyright © Jillian Lin 2016
Illustrations © Shi Meng 2016

Photo of scroll: © Kir (depositphotos.com)
Photo of shrine: © Bernard Gagnon (Wikimedia)
Photo of Dutch surrender: © Thijs Haarhuis (Wikimedia)
Photo of statue in Fujian: © Gisling (Wikimedia)
Photo of statue with mother: © Koika (Wikimedia)

Made in the USA
Columbia, SC
25 January 2022